# By Any Other Name

## Name

## A Book of Roses

DOUBLEDAY

New York   London   Toronto   Sydney   Auckland

PUBLISHED BY DOUBLEDAY

a division of Bantam Doubleday Dell Publishing Group, Inc.

666 Fifth Avenue, New York, New York 10103

DOUBLEDAY and the portrayal of an anchor with a
dolphin are trademarks of Doubleday, a division of
Bantam Doubleday Dell Publishing Group, Inc.

Library of Congress Cataloging-in-Publication Data
By any other name.
1. Roses—Pictorial works.   2. Roses—Quotations,
maxims, etc.   3. Gardens—Pictorial works.
SB411.3.B9   1990        635.9'33372'0222        89-25739
ISBN 0-385-41351-3

Produced by Smallwood and Stewart
Edited by Linda Sunshine
Designed by Dirk Kaufman

Printed in Singapore        May 1990
First Edition

NOTICE: Every effort has been made to locate the copyright
owners of the material used in this book. Please let us know
if an error has been made, and we will make any necessary
changes in subsequent printings.

*What's in a name? That which we call a rose*
*By any other name would smell as sweet.*

William Shakespeare

*Romeo and Juliet*

II, ii, 43

# INTRODUCTION

*The Rose, wherein, the Word Divine makes itself flesh . . .*

Dante

Throughout the ages, the rose has been linked to the goddesses of beauty and love. Rearranging the letters of the word "rose," we get "Eros," the god of love. The Ancients believed that the white rose was stained red by the blood of Venus when her fingers caught on its thorns as she was rushing to keep a tryst with Adonis. Cupid was said to have bribed Harpocrates, the god of silence, with the rose to prevent him from revealing the love affairs carried on by Venus. (Hence the rose also came to be associated with secrecy; confidential meetings were held *sub rosa*, beneath a symbol of a rose.)

In fact, the rose is the oldest domesticated flower known to man; fossil remains indicate that it existed thirty-five million years ago. The rose has been cultivated in Persia for at least 5,000 years. Rose decorations are found on jewelry and ornaments from the Minoan civilization, about 2800 B.C.

The Romans were extravagant in their devotion to the rose. Boxes at their games were garlanded with roses; rose petals perfumed their baths and were showered on guests at lavish banquets. Cleopatra once ordered a fragrant carpet, twenty inches deep, to welcome the arrival of her Roman lover.

After the fall of the Roman empire, rose cultivation was

continued by Benedictine monks and, as the excesses of the Romans were forgotten, the flower became the emblem of Christianity. At the same time under Islam, in enclosed gardens from the Alhambra in Spain to Kashmir, the rose was celebrated as a symbol of perfection. Later, traders and plant hunters brought back new roses from their travels. Most of our popular varieties today—Teas and Hybrid Teas, for example—originated in China and Asia. There, as in the West, roses were highly valued. Rose oil—attar of roses—was a precious fragrance of kings and the most wealthy.

Thus, in the international language of flowers, in poetry, literature, art and legend, the immortal rose has always been celebrated as a symbol of purity and goodness, and a messenger of tenderness and love.

 The Rosa Mariae, the Rose of Jericho, was believed by the pilgrims to the Holy Sepulchre to have sprung up at each resting-place on the flight into Egypt. It was said to have blossomed for the first Christmas, to have closed at the Crucifixion, and reopened on Easter Day.

Abu Zacaria, 12th Century

It is not the least of the tokens of the royalty and dominion of the rose, that the choicest of the sensations which we call color is called by its name. We use it to describe a sunset sky or the tinting of a baby's finger-tips; and even the innumerable variations of shades and dyes of damasks and velvet and precious silken stuffs which commend their tints to human eyes, *rose-color* describes, and the flower mingles its remembrance with the loveliest of them all.

Candace Wheeler

*Plant Poetry*

trange that such a little Rose should
live on for well-nigh half a century, calmly
putting forth its leaf and bloom summer
after summer, whilst so many of the men
and women who knew it once have passed
away. It somehow makes me think of the
old monk, pointing to the frescoes on his
convent walls and saying, *These are realities,*
*we are the shadows.*

E.O. Boyle

*Diary*

*L*ike the rose

*I, too, was careless in the morning dews . . .*

Edith Sitwell

"A Song at Morning"

# *painting the roses*

A large rose-tree stood near the entrance of the garden: the roses growing on it were white, but there were three gardeners at it, busily painting them red.     Alice thought this a very curious thing, and she went nearer to watch them . . .

"Would you tell me, please," said Alice, a little timidly, "why are you painting those roses?"

Five and Seven said nothing, but looked at Two. Two began, in a low voice, "Why, the fact is, you see, Miss, this here ought to have been a *red* rose-tree, and we put a white one in by mistake; and, if the Queen was to find it out, we should all have our heads cut off, you know. So you see, Miss, we're doing our best, afore she comes, to —"        At this moment, Five, who had been anxiously looking across the garden, called out "The Queen! The Queen!" and the three gardeners instantly threw themselves flat on their faces . . .

When the procession came opposite to Alice, they all stopped and looked at her, and the Queen said, severely, "Who is this?" She said it to the Knave of Hearts, who only bowed and smiled in reply.

"Idiot!" said the Queen, tossing her head impatiently; and, turning to Alice, she went on: "What's your name, child?"

"My name is Alice, so please your majesty," said Alice very politely; but she added, to herself, "Why they're only a pack of cards, after all. I needn't be afraid of them!"

"And who are *these?*" said the Queen, pointing to the three gardeners who were lying round the rose-tree; for, you see, as they were lying on their faces, and the pattern on their backs was the same as the rest of the pack, she could not tell whether they were gardeners, or soldiers, or three of her own children . . .

And then, turning to the rose-tree, she went on, "What *have* you been doing here?"

"May it please your Majesty," said Two, in a very humble tone, going down on one knee as he spoke, "we were trying—"

"*I* see!" said the Queen, who had meanwhile been examining the roses. "Off with their heads!"

Lewis Carroll
*Alice's Adventures in Wonderland*

*And I think of roses, roses,*

*White and red, in the wide six-hundred-foot greenhouses,*

*And my father standing astride the cement benches,*

*Lifting me high over the four-foot stems, the Mrs. Russells,*
 *and his own elaborate hybrids,*

*And how those flowerheads seemed to flow toward me, to beckon*
 *me, only a child, out of myself.*

 *What need for heaven, then,*

*With that man, and those roses?*

Theodore Roethke

*The Rose*

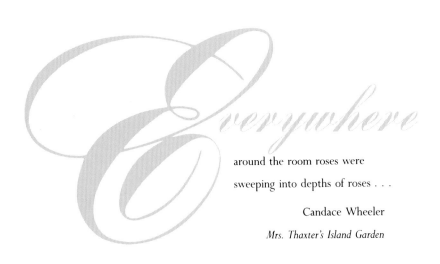

*Everywhere* around the room roses were
sweeping into depths of roses . . .

Candace Wheeler

*Mrs. Thaxter's Island Garden*

## *Rose Pot-pourri*

To a basin of dried scented roses add a
handful of dried knotted Marjoram, lemon
thyme, Rosemary, Lavender flowers all
well dried, the rind of one lemon and one
orange dried to powder, six dried bay
leaves, half an ounce of bruised cloves, a
teaspoon of Allspice. Mix well together
and stir occasionally.

Dated 1895

### THE ROSE FAMILY

*The rose is a rose,*
*And was always a rose.*
*But the theory now goes*
*That the apple's a rose,*
*And the pear is, and so's*
*The plum, I suppose.*
*The dear only knows*
*what will next prove a rose.*
*You, of course, are a rose—*
*But were always a rose.*

Robert Frost

## THE LANGUAGE OF THE ROSE

Austrian Rose . . . Thou Art All that Is Lovely.

Boule de Neige Rose . . . Just for Thee.

Burgundy Rose . . . Simplicity and Beauty.

Cabbage Rose . . . Ambassador of Love.

Campion Rose . . . Deserving of My Love.

Carolina Rose . . . Love Can Be Dangerous.

China Rose . . . Grace or Beauty, Ever Fresh.

Christmas Rose . . . Relieve My Anxiety.

Daily Rose . . . I Aspire to Thy Smile.

Damask Rose . . . Translucent Complexion.

Deep-red Rose . . . Bashful Shame.

Dog Rose . . . Pleasure Mixed with Pain.

Faded Rose . . . Beauty Is Fleeting.

Gloire de Dijon Rose . . . Messenger of Love.

Hundred-leaved Rose . . . Pride.

Japanese Rose . . . Beauty Is Your Sole Attraction.

John Hopper Rose . . . Encouragement.

La France Rose . . . Meet Me by Moonlight.

Maiden Blush Rose . . . If You Love Me, You'll Discover It.

Monteflora Rose . . . Grace.

Moss Rose . . . Voluptuous Love.

Mundi Rose . . . Variety.

Musk Rose . . . Capricious Beauty.

Nephitos Rose . . . Infatuation.

Provence Rose . . . My Heart Is in Flames.

Red Rose . . . Love.

Red Rosebud . . . Pure and Lovely.

Single Rose . . . Simplicity.

Spray of White Rosebuds . . . Secrecy.

Thornless Rose . . . Early Attachment.

Unique Rose . . . Do Not Call Me Beautiful.

White and Red Rose Together . . . Unity.

White Rose . . . I Am Worthy of You.

White Rosebud . . . Too Young to Love.

Wreath of Roses . . . Beauty and Virtue Rewarded.

Yellow Rose . . . Infidelity.

York & Lancaster Rose . . . War.

We all know persons who are affected for better or for worse by certain odours . . . Over and over again I have experienced the quieting influence of Rose scent upon a disturbed state of mind, feeling the troubled condition smoothing out before I realized that Roses were in the room, or near at hand.

Louise Beebe Wilder

*Pleasures of the Nose*

Thus we have made a garden on the smallest plot, or on a great estate. And there the rose will thrive on Love, however mean its offering, rewarding many times its unremitting toil.

S. C. Bradford

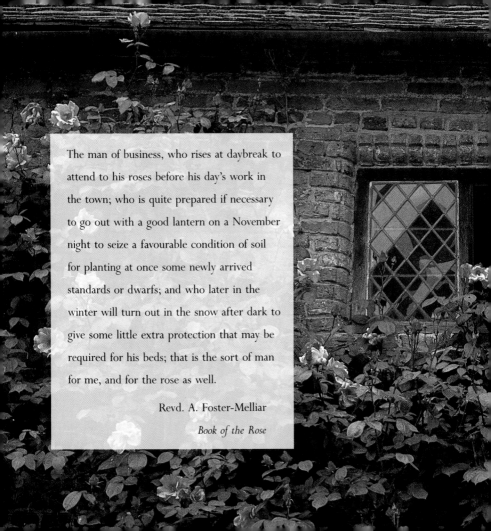

The man of business, who rises at daybreak to attend to his roses before his day's work in the town; who is quite prepared if necessary to go out with a good lantern on a November night to seize a favourable condition of soil for planting at once some newly arrived standards or dwarfs; and who later in the winter will turn out in the snow after dark to give some little extra protection that may be required for his beds; that is the sort of man for me, and for the rose as well.

Revd. A. Foster-Melliar

*Book of the Rose*

## ROSE PETAL CONSERVE

Red roses make the best conserve and they must be gathered when fully open but before they begin to fade. Cut off the white heels for these have a bitter flavor. Dry the petals on sieves out of direct sunlight and if possible in a draft as they then dry quickly. When dried, put a pound of petals into a muslin bag and plunge for a moment into boiling water. Drain well. Have ready a syrup made with a pound of loaf sugar and very little water. Add two tablespoons of orange-flower water. Put in the petals and cook until the conserve is very thick. Keep on pressing the petals under the syrup. Pour into small jars and cover down securely as for jam.

This conserve has a most delicious flavor and the more richly scented the roses, the better the flavor.

## HOW TO PERFUME GLOVES

Take Rose-water and Angelica-water; add the
powder of Cloves, Ambergreece, Musk and Lignum
Aloes. Boil, then hang them in the sun to dry,
turning them often. Thus, three times wet and dry
them. Otherwise, take Rose-water and wet your
Gloves; hang them up till almost dry. Take half an
ounce of Benjamin and grind with Almond oil; rub
on the Gloves till almost dry and then hang them up
to dry or let them dry on your bosom. And, so,
after, use them with pleasure.

Gervase Markham

*The English Housewife of 1675*

*June of the iris and the rose.*
*The rose not English as we fondly think.*
*Anacreon and Bion sang the rose;*
*And Rhodes the isle whose very name means rose*
*Struck roses on her coins;*
*Pliny made lists and Roman libertines*
*Made wreaths to wear among the flutes and wines;*
*The young Crusaders found the Syrian rose*
*Springing from Saracenic quoins,*
*And China opened her shut gate*
*To let her roses through, and Persian shrines*
*Of poetry and painting gave the rose.*

Vita Sackville-West

## MUSK ROSE WATER

Take two handfuls of your Musk
Rose leaves, put them into
about a quart of fair water and a
quarter of a pound of sugar, let
this stand and steep about half
an hour, then take your water
and flowers and pour them out
of one vessel into another till
such time as the water hath
taken the scent and taste of the
flowers, then set it in a cool
place a-cooling and you will find
it a most excellent scent-water.

William Rabisha
*The Whole Body of Cookery Dissected,*
*1675*

*"Flaming Beauty"*

*(Hybrid Tea)*

*"Complicata"*

*(Gallica)*

*"Granada"*

*(Hybrid Tea)*

*"Apricot Nectar"*

*(Floribunda)*

*Oh! No man knows*
*Through what wild centuries*
*Roves back the rose.*

Walter de la Mare

# *the secret garden*

She was standing *inside* the secret garden.

It was the sweetest, most mysterious-looking

place anyone could imagine. 🌷 The high

walls which shut it in were covered with the

leafless stems of climbing roses, which were so

thick that they were matted together. Mary

Lennox knew they were roses because she had

seen a great many roses in India. All the ground

was covered with grass of wintry brown, and

out of it grew clumps of bushes which were

surely rose-bushes if they were alive.

There were numbers of standard roses which had so spread their branches that they were like little trees. There were other trees in the garden, and one of the things that made the place look strangest and loveliest was that climbing roses had run all over them and swung down long tendrils which made light swaying curtains, and here and there they had caught at each other or at a far-reaching branch and had crept from one tree to another and made lovely bridges of themselves. There were neither leaves nor roses on them now, and Mary did not know whether they were dead or alive, but their thin grey or brown branches and sprays looked like a sort of hazy mantle spreading over everything, walls, and trees, and even brown grass, where they had fallen from their fastenings, and run along the ground. It was this hazy tangle from tree to tree which made it look so mysterious. Mary had thought it must be different from other gardens which had not been left all by themselves so long; and, indeed, it was different from any other place she had ever seen in her life . . . and she felt she had found a world all her own.

Frances Hodgson Burnett
*The Secret Garden*

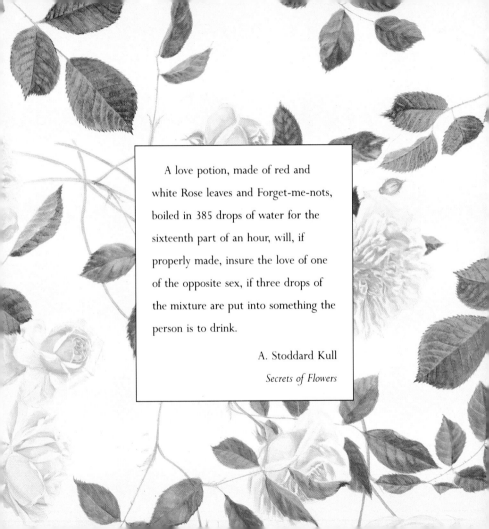

A love potion, made of red and white Rose leaves and Forget-me-nots, boiled in 385 drops of water for the sixteenth part of an hour, will, if properly made, insure the love of one of the opposite sex, if three drops of the mixture are put into something the person is to drink.

A. Stoddard Kull

*Secrets of Flowers*

There should be beds of Roses, banks of Roses, bowers of Roses, hedges of Roses, edgings of Roses, pillars of Roses, arches of Roses, fountains of Roses, baskets of Roses, vistas and alleys of the Rose.

Dean Hole

*A Book About Roses*

# roses in june

Tess wished to abridge her visit as much as possible; but the young man was pressing, and she consented to accompany him. He conducted her around the lawns, and flower-beds, and conservatories . . . and then the two passed round to the rose-trees, whence he gathered blossoms and gave her to put in her bosom. She obeyed like one in a dream, and when she could affix no more he himself tucked a bud or two into her hat, and heaped her basket with others in the prodigality of his bounty. . . .

Tess went down the hill to Trantridge Cross, and inattentively waited to take her seat in the van returning from Chaseborough to Shaston. She did not know what the other occupants said to her as she entered, though she answered

them; and when they had started anew she rode
along with an inward and not an outward eye.

One among her fellow-travellers addressed
her more pointedly than any had spoken
before: 'Why, you be quite a posy! And such
roses in early June!'

Then she became aware of the spectacle she
presented to their surprised vision: roses at her
breast; roses in her hat, roses and strawberries
in her basket to the brim. She blushed,
and said confusedly that the flowers had been

given to her. When the passengers were not looking she stealthily removed the more prominent blooms from her hat and placed them in the basket, where she covered them with her handkerchief. Then she fell to reflecting again, and in looking downwards, a thorn of the rose remaining in her breast accidentally pricked her chin. Like all the cottagers in Blackmoor Vale, Tess was steeped in fancies and prefigurative superstitions; she thought this an ill omen—the first she had noticed that day.

Thomas Hardy
*Tess of the d'Urbervilles*

So, if it is to be a rose-garden, do not choose those stunted, unnatural earth-loving strains, which have nothing of vigour and wildness in them, nor banish other flowers which may do homage to the beauty of a rose as courtiers to a queen. Let climbing roses drop in a veil from the terrace and smother with flower-spangled embroidery the garden walls, run riot over vaulted arcades, clamber up lofty obelisks of leaf-tangled trellis, twine themselves round the pillars of a rose-roofed

temple, where little avalanches of sweetness shall rustle down at a touch and the dusty gold of the sunshine shall mingle with the summer snow of the flying petals. Let them leap in a great bow or fall in a creamy cataract to a foaming pool of flowers. In the midst of the garden set a statue of Venus with a great bloom trained to her hand, or of Flora, her cornucopia overflowing with white rosettes, or a tiny basin where leaden *amorini* seated upon the margin are fishing with trailing buds.

Sir George Sitwell
*On the Making of Gardens*

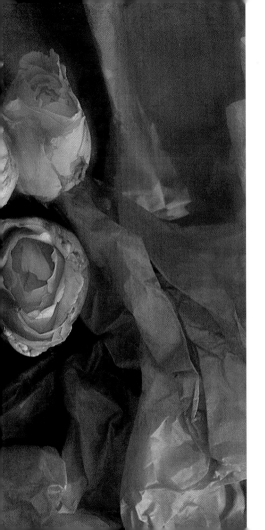

## ESSENCE OF ROSES

Layer rose petals in a large stone
jar with sea salt and press the layers
well down. When the jar is full, seal
it and stand it in a cool, shaded
place for 40 days.

Turn the contents of the jar into
a cloth and strain off the liquid,
squeezing the cloth gently to ex-
tract it all. Put the essence into
glass bottles until they are two-
thirds full. Seal and leave to stand
in the sun for 25 to 30 days to
purify the essence.

Ann Mayhew

*The Rose: Myth, Folklore and Legend*

Our highest assurance of the goodness of providence seems to me to rest in the flowers. All other things, our desires, our food, are really necessary for our existence in the first instance. But this rose is an extra. Its smell and its colour are an embellishment of life, not a condition of it. It is only goodness which gives extras, and so I say again that we have much to hope for from the flowers.

Sir Arthur Conan Doyle
"The Naval Treaty"
*The Memoirs of Sherlock Holmes*

# *a cut rose*

One morning, as he was cutting roses in his garden, Florentino Ariza could not resist the temptation of taking one to [Fermina Daza] on his next visit. It was a difficult problem in the language of flowers because she was a recent widow. A red rose, symbol of flaming passion,

might offend her mourning. Yellow roses, which in
another language were the flowers of good
fortune, were an expression of jealousy in the
common vocabulary. He had heard of the black
roses of Turkey, which was perhaps the most
appropriate, but he had not been able to obtain
any for acclimatization in his patio. After
much thought he risked a white rose, which he
liked less than the others because it was insipid
and mute: it did not say anything. At the last
minute, in case Fermina Daza was suspicious

enough to attribute some meaning to it, he removed the thorns.

It was well received as a gift with no hidden intentions, and the Tuesday ritual was enriched, so that when he would arrive with the white rose, the vase with water was ready in the center of the tea table. One Tuesday, as he placed the rose in the vase, he said in an apparently casual manner:

"In our day it was camellias, not roses."

"That is true," she said, "but the intention was different, and you know it."

Gabriel García Marquez
*Love in the Time of Cholera*

*I*n earlier times, household linens were laundered, then rinsed in water perfumed with herbs or flowers. To prepare your own rose water, fill a saucepan with the scented petals of freshly picked roses. Pour over water to cover them, and simmer for just a few minutes. Allow the rose water to cool, then strain through muslin into a bottle. It may be refrigerated for about a week. Any scented rose is suitable for rose water, the more perfumed the better.

## A Fancy from Fontenelle

### "De memoires de roses on n'a point vu mourir le Jardinier"

*The Rose in the garden slipped her bud,*
*And she laughed in the pride of her youthful blood,*
*As she thought of the Gardener standing by—*
*"He is old,—so old! And he soon must die!"*

*The full Rose waxed in the warm June air,*
*And she spread and spread till her heart lay bare;*
*And she laughed once more as she heard his tread—*
*"He is older now! He will soon be dead!"*

*But the breeze of the morning blew, and found*
*That the leaves of the blown Rose strewed the ground;*
*And he came at noon, that Gardener old,*
*And he raked them gently under the mould.*

*And I wove the thing to a random rhyme,*
*For the Rose is Beauty, the Gardener, Time.*

Austin Dobson

## CANDIED ROSE PETALS

Slightly beat one egg-white in a small bowl.
Sprinkle a layer of sugar on a small plate. Dip
rose petals and leaves first in egg-white and then
in sugar so they are coated on both sides. Dry on
rack. Store dried petals and leaves on waxpaper,
each layer separated by paper toweling. Use on
candy tray, as garnish for fruit cup, as decoration
on cakes or as border for cake plate.

Matthew A. R. Bassity

*The Magic World of Roses*

How simple and rustic . . . would seem
the dog-roses which, in a few weeks time,
would be climbing the same hillside path
in the heat of the sun, dressed in the
smooth silk of their blushing pink bodices,
which would be undone and scattered by
the first breath of wind.

Marcel Proust
*Swann's Way*

## ONE PERFECT ROSE

A single flow'r he sent me, since we met.
    All tenderly his messenger he chose;
Deep-hearted, pure, with scented dew still wet—
    One perfect rose.

I knew the language of the floweret;
    "My fragile leaves," it said, "his heart enclose."
Love long has taken for his amulet
    One perfect rose.

Why is it no one ever sent yet
    One perfect limousine, do you suppose?
Ah no, it's always just my luck to get
    One perfect rose.

Dorothy Parker

Abu Zacaria (864-925), Persian physician and philosopher

Anderson, Hans Christian (1805-75), Danish poet, novelist, and writer of fairy tales

Bullet, Gerald (1893-1958), English writer and critic

Burnett, Frances Hodgson (1849-1924), American writer, known for her children's books

Carroll, Lewis (Charles Dodgson; 1832-98), English writer and mathematician

de la Mare, Walter (1873-1956), English poet and novelist

Dobson, Austin (1840-1921), English poet, essayist, and biographer

Doyle, Sir Arthur Conan (1859-1930), English writer; creator of Sherlock Holmes

Emerson, Ralph Waldo (1803-82), American poet and essayist

Frost, Robert (1874-1963), American poet

Hole, Samuel Reynolds (Dean; 1819-1904), English rosarian and writer

Markham, Gervase (1568-1637), English writer on horses and country life

Márquez, Gabriel García (b. 1928), Colombian novelist and short-story writer

Moore, Thomas (1779-1852), Irish poet

Parker, Dorothy (1893-1967), American writer of satiric short-stories and verses

Proust, Marcel (1871-1922), French novelist

Roethke, Theodore (1908-53), American poet

Sackville-West, Vita (Victoria; 1892-1962), English writer

Shakespeare, William (1564-1616), English dramatist and poet

Sitwell, Sir George (1860-1943), English landscape gardener and writer

Wheeler, Candace (1827-1923), American fabric designer; writer of books on design

Wilder, Louise Beebe (1878-1938), American writer of gardening books

# ACKNOWLEDGMENTS

"The Rose Family," by Robert Frost, is from *The Poetry of Robert Frost*, edited by Edward Connery Lathem. Copyright 1928, © 1969 by Holt, Rinehart and Winston, Inc. Copyright © 1956 by Robert Frost. Reprinted by arrangement with Henry Holt and Company, Inc.

"Love Potion" from *Secrets of Flowers*, by A.S. Kull. Copyright © 1966 by The Stephen Greene Press. All rights reserved. Reprinted by permission of Viking Penguin, a division of Penguin Books USA, Inc.

*Love In The Time of Cholera*, by Gabriel García Márquez, translation from Spanish by Edith Grossman. Copyright © 1988 by Alfred A. Knopf. Reprinted by permission of the publisher.

"Essences of Roses," by Ann Mayhew, is from *The Rose: Myth, Folklore and Legend*. Copyright © 1979 by Ann Mayhew. All rights reserved. First published in London by New English Library. Published in the U.S. by Walker and Company.

"One Perfect Rose" from *The Portable Dorothy Parker* by Dorothy Parker. Copyright 1926, renewed 1954 by Dorothy Parker. All rights reserved. Reprinted by permission of Viking Penguin, a division of Penguin Books USA, Inc.

"The Rose," copyright © 1963 by Beatrice Roethke, Administratrix of the Estate of Theodore Roethke. From *The Collected Poems of Theodore Roethke* by Theodore Roethke. Used by permission of Doubleday, a division of Bantam, Doubleday, Dell Publishing Group, Inc.

# ART CREDITS

Jacket: TGPL Laszlo Puskas; 1 TGPL Vaughan Fleming; 6-7 Derek Harris; 12 Boys Syndication; 13 Linda Burgess/Insight; 15 Boys/JH; 17 Boys/JH; 18 Wendi Schneider; 21 TGPL Gill Marais; 29 Tania Midgely; 30-31 TGPL Perdereau-Thomas; 33 Nana Watanabe; 34 Linda Burgess/Insight; 36-37 Wendi Schneider; 38 Linda Burgess/Insight; 42 Boys Syndication; 45 Sandra Eisner; 46-47 TGPL Gary Rogers; 48 Linda Burgess/Insight; 50 Beth Galton; 54-55 TGPL Gill Marais; 56-57 Derek Harris; 59 Linda Burgess/Insight; 60 TGPL Gary Rogers; 66 TGPL Brigitte Thomas; 73 & 74 Tania Midgely; 76 TGPL Gary Rogers; 78 Boys/JH; 80 TGPL Elizabeth Strauss; 84 TGPL Laszlo Puskas; 86-87 TGPL Gary Rogers; 88 Linda Burgess/Insight; 91 Jacqui Hurst; 93 Wendi Schneider; 96 TGPL Vaughan Fleming.

TGPL: The Garden Picture Library
Boys/JH: Boys Syndication/Jacqui Hurst

Paper on pages 20-21 reproduced by permission of Melissa Neufeld Inc., PO Box 794, Diablo, CA 94528
Paper on pages 64-65 reproduced by permission of The Gordon Fraser Gallery, Inc.